LONDON ABC

ILLUSTRATED BY

BEN HAWKES

PICTURE CORGI

LONDON

A   B   C

A   PICTURE   CORGI   BOOK

978   0   552   56674   2

First published in Great Britain by Doubleday,
an imprint of Random House Children's Publishers UK
A Random House Group Company Doubleday edition
published 2012 Picture Corgi edition published 2012

3   5   7   9   10   8   6   4

Picture Corgi Books are published by
RANDOM   HOUSE   CHILDREN'S   PUBLISHERS   UK
61-63   Uxbridge   Road,   London   W5   5SA
w w w . r a n d o m h o u s e c h i l d r e n s . c o . u k
w w w . r a n d o m h o u s e . c o . u k
Addresses for companies within The Random House
Group Limited can be found at:
www.randomhouse.co.uk/offices.htm
THE RANDOM HOUSE GROUP Limited
Reg.   No.   954009
A CIP catalogue record
for this book
is available
from the
British Library.
Printed in China

WELCOME TO LONDON!

London is one of the most famous and iconic capital cities in the world. It is busy, bustling and full of treasures for you to discover. It's a centre for fashion, films and food, business, the arts and entertainment. Plus it's filled with countless museums, galleries, theatres, sporting grounds, shops, markets, parks and palaces. We are excited to show you some of these in this ABC!

Most of all London is full of stories — its history stretches back over 2,000 years, and it has been immortalised in hundreds of books, TV series and movies: from Dickens's Victorian London, to the London of Sherlock Holmes, Mary Poppins and Doctor Who.

We can't wait for YOU to explore London and start your own story. There are so many ways to discover the city: on foot, finding hidden side streets; on the underground (do you know which colour is for which line?); on red London buses or in black cabs. Remember to take care crossing the road and always have an adult with you!

And don't forget to take this book with you too. On each page there are lots of things for you to spot beginning with that letter. Some are London things and some aren't! See if you can spot them all, and then turn to the back of the book to check your answers. We've also suggested some other London landmarks for you to seek out. And see if you can spot what our lost little penguin friend is up to as well.

Have fun exploring the London in this book, and the real-life one outside your door . . .

A IS FOR AQUARIUM

B IS FOR

BIG BEN

C IS FOR

CROWN JEWELS

E IS FOR **EYE**

H IS FOR

HYDE PARK

FREE HUGS

I IS FOR

I ♥ LONGON

chocolate VANILLA STRAWBERRY

J IS FOR **JUBILEE!**

K IS FOR **K**EW

L IS FOR **LORD MAYOR'S SHOW**

Q IS FOR QUEEN

chocolate VANILLA STRAWBERRY

QUIET PLEASE

The Red Rose

R IS FOR ROAST DINNER

S IS FOR **STADIUM**

T IS FOR

TOWER BRIDGE

CHAPMAN 2

MACDONALD 2

W IS FOR WIMBLEDON

Y IS FOR

YOGA

YIPPEE!!!!!

DID YOU SPOT?

A IS ALSO FOR: Anchor, apple, aquanaut

B IS ALSO FOR: Bearskin, bicycle, black cab, boat, bobby, bridge, Buckingham Palace, bus

C IS ALSO FOR: Camera, case, cat burglar, crown, cushion

D IS ALSO FOR: Dog, door, doorknob

E IS ALSO FOR: Elephant, English flag (St George)

F IS ALSO FOR: Fedora, fire bucket, fire engine, fire hose, firemen, fish, football

G IS ALSO FOR: Gallery, gentleman, Gherkin, glasses

H IS ALSO FOR: Hair, hat, hedge, helicopter, helmet, horse, hot dog, hugs

I IS ALSO FOR: Ice cream, ice-cream van, insect, iris, iron gates

J IS ALSO FOR: Jelly, jug, juggler, juggling balls

K IS ALSO FOR: Kate, King (to be), kiss, kite, kitten, knitter

L IS ALSO FOR: Ladder, lamp post

M IS ALSO FOR: Map, monkey, monocle, monster, moustache, museum

N IS ALSO FOR: National Gallery, necklace, newspaper, newsstand

O IS ALSO FOR: Octopus, onion, ostrich

P IS ALSO FOR: Pear, penguin, people, phone box, pigeon, pizza restaurant, post box, poster

Q IS ALSO FOR: Queue, quiche, "quiet please" sign, quilt

R IS ALSO FOR: Rain, reading glasses, red wine, roast beef, roast potatoes, rose, royals

S IS ALSO FOR: Sailor, screen, sky, sportsmen, sprinters, stands, sun

T IS ALSO FOR: Taxi, Thames, tiger, Tower of London, traffic, tugboat

U IS ALSO FOR: Ukulele, umbrella, uniforms, Union Jack

V IS ALSO FOR: Van, video camera

W IS ALSO FOR: Wasp, wellies, whites, worm

X IS ALSO FOR: X marks the spot, x-ray, xylophone

Y IS ALSO FOR: Yawn, yellow, yoga, yoghurt, yo-yo

Z IS ALSO FOR: Zebra, zookeeper

LONDON LANDMARKS FEATURED IN THIS BOOK

Big Ben

The British Museum

Buckingham Palace

Downing Street

The Gherkin

The Houses of Parliament

Hyde Park

Kew Gardens

King's Cross Station

Leicester Square

The London Aquarium

The London Eye

London Zoo

The National Gallery

Nelson's Column

The Olympic Park

Oxford Circus

Piccadilly Circus

Regent's Park

St Paul's Cathedral

The Serpentine

Shakespeare's Globe

The Statue of Eros

The Thames

Tower Bridge

The Tower of London

Trafalgar Square

Westminster Bridge

Wimbledon

OTHER LANDMARKS FOR YOU TO VISIT

The Albert Memorial

Apsley House

The Bank of England

The Barbican

Battersea Power Station

The British Library

Broadcasting House

Carnaby Street

Charing Cross

City Hall

Cleopatra's Needle

Covent Garden

Cutty Sark

Fortnum & Mason

Foyles

Green Park

Hamleys

Hampstead Heath

Hampton Court

Harrods

HMS Belfast

Highgate Cemetery

Horse Guards Parade

Imperial War Museum

Kensington Palace

Liberty

Little Venice

Lloyd's of London

The London Dungeon

The London Transport Museum

Lord's Cricket Ground

Madame Tussauds

The Mall

Mansion House

Marble Arch

The Millennium Bridge

The Monument

The Museum of London

The National Maritime Museum

The National Portrait Gallery

The National Theatre

The Natural History Museum

The O2

The Old Bailey

The Oxo Tower

Paddington Station

Peter Pan in Kensington Gardens

Portobello Market

The Ritz Hotel

The Royal Albert Hall

The Royal Observatory

The Royal Opera House

The Science Museum

Selfridges

Smithfield Market

Spitalfields Market

South Bank

The Southbank Centre

Southwark Cathedral

Speaker's Corner

St James's Palace

St James's Park

Tate Britain

Tate Modern

Theatreland

Twickenham

The V & A

Wembley Stadium

Westminster Abbey